LLANELLI POSTCARDS OF YESTERYEAR

Brian Cripps

First impression—November 1994

ISBN 1 85902 193 X

Printed by
J. D. Lewis & Sons,
Gomer Press,
Llandysul, Dyfed

LLANELLI POSTCARDS OF YESTERYEAR

Dear Reader,

Eight years ago I published my first collection of Llanelli postcards. The volume was so well received that it prompted me to assemble a second selection of Llanelli and district postcards.

To those who know the area, some views will be familiar but others, reproductions of rare cards, will be unfamiliar to all but a few readers. There is no doubt that some photographs will jog memories and I would be pleased to hear from anyone who can provide additional information relating to the illustrations depicted.

To help readers and collectors, a guide is included to indicate how each picture rates as regards its known availability in the postcard market. Additional details are provided on local photographers and publishers who have captured Llanelli's rich historical past on film.

I trust you enjoy this latest collection.

A map of the area is also produced on page x.

BRIAN CRIPPS
LLANELLI, 1994

A BRIEF HISTORY OF LLANELLI POSTCARDS

In Britain, postcards were first put on sale in October 1870 and were published by the security printers, Messrs De La Rue Company Limited. Between 1870 and 1894 as many as 30 different types of card appeared but in 1894 viewcards were published for the first time and these proved an immediate success. Picture postcards became big business and could be sent anywhere in the U.K. for the cost of ½d (0.21p).

Picture postcards of Llanelli prior to 1900 are virtually unrecorded. The first cards to appear were the product of the three leading postcard publishers, Messrs Raphael Tuck, John Evelyn Wrench and Francis Frith, and between 1902 and 1930 view cards of Llanelli, Burry Port, Pembrey and villages in the Gwendraeth valley sold in vast quantities, especially in shops such as Boots the Chemist in Stepney Street, Llanelli. Soon, several locally-based photographers earned good reputations for their superb photos which were published in card form, and many people began to take an interest in collecting postcards. Frank James Anthony (1877-1947) born in Llanelli, of an old Llanelli family, was a particularly gifted photographer. He spent his early years at Royston, Cambridge and at Tenby in Pembrokeshire where he befriended the great Tenby photographer, H. Mortimer Allen, whose first studio, built by his famous father, Charles Smith Allen, overlooked the harbour. About 1905 F. J. Anthony opened his Victoria Photographic Studio at 3 Vaughan Street, Llanelli, near to where Boots the Chemist is today. His popular portrait photos soon gave way to the far more profitable business of selling local picture postcards. His cards sold well because the published results were of top quality and included interesting street scenes and photographs of visiting VIPs. In 1939 he moved his studio to Cowell House in Cowell Street and to this day the large glass-covered extension built at the rear of Cowell House to house his

Frank James Anthony (Snr)
(1877-1947)

studio is still visible. Following F. J. Anthony's retirement in 1947 the business was taken over by a Mr Charles Barker who subsequently moved to London in 1952.

The following local photographers/publishers, operating during the first three decades of the century, have also left a legacy of postcards now sought by today's collectors:

Ernest T. Bush, Burry Port and Llanelli
John Vaughan Evans, 6 Cowell Street, Llanelli
David John, 44 Stepney Street, Llanelli
John Marker, Tobacconist, 7A Stepney Street, Llanelli
H. Mainwaring, 30 Station Road, Llanelli
Thomas Cards, 38 Thomas Street, Llanelli
The Eurwedd Series, 14 Market Street, Llanelli
Charles Snook, Newsagent, Station Road, Burry Port
Hoare Bros., Cambrian Studio, Burry Port
Excelsior Photo Company, Carmarthen
Boots the Chemist, Stepney Street, Llanelli
Ernie Griffiths, Llanelli
Gascoigne, Stationer, Llanelli
J. Harper, Burry Port
H. Williams, Newsagent, Burry Port
W. T. Perrott, Stationer, Burry Port
F. J. Morgan, Burry Port
W. Yorath Davies, Burry Port

It is important to note that these early photographers took large format photographs: either quarto (10″ × 8″), whole plate (8½″ × 6½″) or half plate (4″ × 6″) and these were then reduced to postcard-size prints measuring 5½″ × 3½″. By enlarging the postcards, one can begin to appreciate how good the original photographs were. Indeed, many contemporary photographers readily admit that these Edwardian black-and-white prints have a quality which cannot be bettered.

Collecting old postcards is now one of the most popular hobbies in the world. The variety of subject matter is huge and most cards sell for between £2.00 and £30.00. Many collectors, however, are only interested in contemporary cards which again feature a wide range of subject matter.

One word of warning to those contemplating taking up the hobby for the first time: once 'hooked' the enthusiasm never seems to diminish. Postcard collecting, or deltiology, is a joy for young and old, and it is entirely appropriate that this collection of Llanelli postcards of yesteryear—which includes reproductions of such classic views as the 1904 train crash, the 1911 rail riots and Amelia Earhart landing in 1928—should be published in 1994, the hundredth anniversary of the picture postcard.

A GUIDE TO THE AVAILABILITY OF LLANELLI POSTCARDS

Class	Availability Rating
1	Very, very rare
2	Rare, difficult to find
3	Scarce
4	Fairly common, but can sometimes be difficult to find
5	Easily found and plentiful
6	Very common, and only worth collecting if in pristine condition.

When collecting cards, the value or selling price is not only governed by its availability (classes 1-6), but also by the condition of the postcard and by the presence of rare postmarks or uncommon stamps. True photographic cards always command a higher value than a printed version of the same card.

ACKNOWLEDGEMENTS

During the past eight years I have been most fortunate in obtaining cards, thanks to the kindness of many acquaintances and friends. In parcticular I thank local residents, many of whom brought cards to my attention during my lecture trips. I also thank many dealers and stamp club colleagues who have helped me to add to my collection. A special thanks also goes to Frank J. Anthony (junior), for his help with details regarding his father's career.

I also kindly thank Mrs Dianne Reyonlds of Felin-foel for her much appreciated assistance and interest. But most of all, I thank my wife, Lorna, who has spent many hours with me at postcard events searching through endless boxes of innumerable Welsh cards for the few Llanelli 'gems' which have made this book possible.

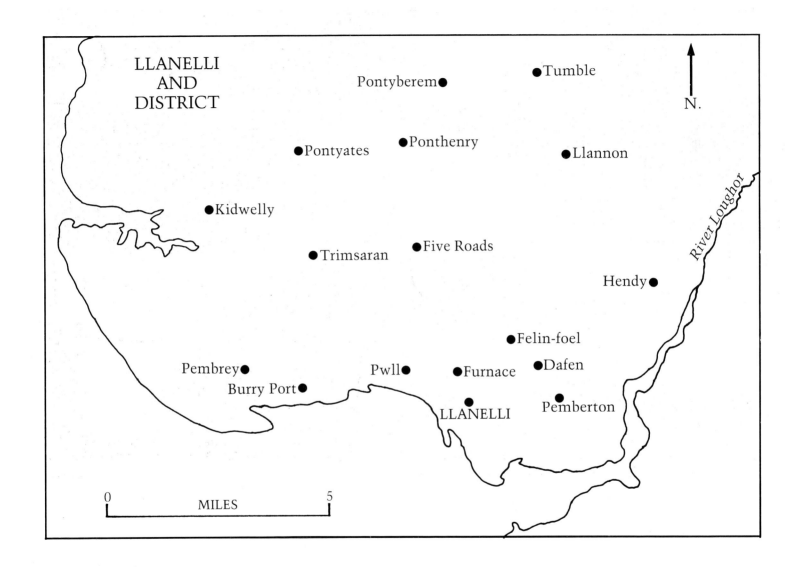

LLANELLI
AND
DISTRICT

N.

Pontyberem●   ●Tumble

●Pontyates   ●Ponthenry   ●Llannon

●Kidwelly

●Trimsaran   ●Five Roads

Hendy●

●Felin-foel

Pembrey●   Pwll●   ●Furnace   ●Dafen

Burry Port●

LLANELLI   ●Pemberton

0   MILES   5

A multiview card of town views by S. H. Gascoigne, *c.* 1915.

A panoramic view of the Town Hall Square. Note the bill-board (right) advertising a Bank Holiday Ritz Dance, *c*. 1956. *Class 4*

Two men cleaning the gas light in Athenaeum Square, *c.* 1902. Note the old buildings in Church Street (left).   *Class 5*

Llanelly Tramways Co. Ltd. horse-drawn tram at the junction of Cowell Street and Murray Street, *c.* 1906. *Class 3*

A viewcard by Vaughan Evans, postmarked 1906. This rare card is an elevated view of buildings around Llanelli's Arcade.

Class 2

F. J. Anthony's view of Trinity Chapel at the junction of New Dock Road and Trinity Road, *c.* 1912.   *Class 5*

A busy view of Stepney Street with No. 10 and No. 11 trams passing each other, *c.* 1913.

Class 4

The old Llanelli Hospital, built 1885. S. H. Gascoigne's view is dated *c.* 1915.

Class 6

Huge crowds in Athenaeum Square. Many people are in their Sunday best for the Stepney-Howard wedding day held in St. Elli's Church, September 1911.

Class 2

St. Elli's Church. This Philco card is dated *c.* 1948.

An interesting view of the York Hotel and Lucania Buildings, *c.* 1932. Note the two old buses (left). *Class 4*

Castle Buildings and Murray Street, free of traffic, *c.* 1909. A cinema now stands on the site of the private garden (left). The photograph is by D. John.

Class 6

Children in fancy dress standing in Coleshill Terrace during carnival week, 1933. The Town Hall stands in the background.
Class 3

Market Street, Llanelly

A rare viewcard of Market Street. Opposite the Telegraph Boy and bicycle (left) stands the Bush Vaults. *Class 2*

St. Joseph's Convent, High School, Llanelly.

A rare London printed card of St Joseph's Convent School in Myrtle Terrace, with pupils in the gardens, *c.* 1906.   *Class 1*

An ivy decorated class-room in St. Joseph's Convent School, *c.* 1906.

Class 1

A Francis Frith viewcard of Town Hall Square, *c.* 1955. Note the bus shelter in Old Frederick Street (right). *Class 6*

Station Road, Llanelly.

A superb view of Station Road, *c.* 1912. In those days it was safe to walk in the road although trams did pose an occasional hazard to pedestrians. This card is by F. J. Anthony.

Class 2

18

A Llanelli tram about to enter the tram depot in Robinson Street, 1930. Trams were replaced by trolley buses in 1932.

Class 1

Victoria Road, Llanelly.

This F. J. Anthony card of Queen Victoria Road is postmarked 1910. Pedestrians found it safe to stroll in mid town streets at the beginning of the century.

Class 3

An aerial view of Llanelli town centre depicting housing in Murray Street, Park Church and the old Town Market, *c.* 1925.　　　　*Class 2*

This card, postmarked June 1911, was published to record the change from horse-drawn to electric trams.　　*Class 4*

Lord Roberts on the occasion of his visit to Llanelli in August 1905. On a rainy day, Earl Roberts unveiled a memorial to local men killed in the Boer War.
Class 5

Lord Roberts's parade passing under a tin archway erected by troops of the 1st V. B. Welch Regiment, 1905.
Class 5

Looted railway trucks being examined by police and troops after the Llanelli strike riots of August 1911. *Class 2*

Probably the finest view ever taken of Llanelli Station, *c.* 1914. It shows the 'Flower Class' 4-4-0 Loco. No. 4151. The Stepney spare motor wheels were manufactured in the building to the left of the station.

Class 1

VAUGHAN STREET AND PUBLIC LIBRARY, LLANELLY.

Tram lines leading down Vaughan Street in the direction of the market entrance located in Stepney Street. This card, postmarked 1937, also depicts the Victoria Photo Studio owned by Frank J. Anthony. It is situated by the parked car. *Class 2*

This 1930s card shows assembled members of the Llanelli Branch of the British Legion. *Class 2*

Stradey Castle, Llanelli. The card, postmarked 1910, is by Raphael Tuck.

Class 6

Established in 1832, the Cambrian Wine and Spirit Vaults was located at the corner of Market Street and Stepney Street. Today it's known as The Barbican.

Class 1

Wounded First World War troops and nursing staff at Stebon Heath School, 1917. A Red Cross Matron is sat next to a Lt. Colonel visiting the convalescing troops.

Class 5

This Valentine Co. card, postmarked 1913, shows two coal hoists and a two-masted brigantine in the North Dock, Llanelli.

Class 5

View of North Dock, Llanelly

Two tug boats and a three-masted barque in the North Dock. The card is postmarked 1915. *Class 5*

Many views exist of Llanelli Town Hall but this photograph also shows the Regal Cinema and Ritz Dance Hall in the background, *c.* 1938.

Class 4

A 1930s card of Capel Als Choir, Llanelli, bound on its annual outing to Tenby. *Class 3*

Stepney Street, largely devoid of vehicular traffic, in 1936. The Llanelli Cinema is situated opposite the York Hotel. *Class 4*

Llanelly Tuesday's A.F.C., 1913-14. Difficult though it may be to believe, there are more soccer teams than rugby teams in Llanelli!

Class 3

A Vaughan Evans postcard, postmarked 1905, depicting the cascade water steps at Swiss Valley.

Class 5

An extremely rare postcard of a Llanelly Corporation steam-driven waggon, August 1926.

Class 1

Coal and cargo ships berthed in the North Dock, Llanelli. The card was published in London, *c.* 1937. *Class 4*

Oh! What a photograph. A rare Frank J. Anthony card portraying the staff of Pugh Bros., Cowell Street, about to depart on a coach trip, *c.* 1912.

Class 1

The popular Parc Howard bowling green. The card is postmarked 1916.

Class 5

40

A band concert in Parc Howard, *c*. 1912. The children are clearly in their Sunday best clothes.

Class 5

Disasters invariably attract onlookers and the October 1904 rail smash was no exception. Five persons were killed in the accident and 38 injured.

Class 3

A heavy-lifting rail crane was called upon to lift the locomotive damaged in the accident in October 1904. *Class 4*

Frenchman Monsieur Salmet signing an autograph for Canon McLoughlin on the cleared Stradey Park cricket pitch on 25 May 1912. The Bleriot monoplane flight was sponsored by the *Daily Mail* newspaper.

Class 1

The main entrance to the Llanelli Girls' Grammar School protected by an anti air-raid wall erected in 1940. *Class 2*

This 1913 card of Old Stepney Street ranks amongst Vaughan Evans's finest photographs.

Class 2

Private houses in Salamanca Road (now Station Road). The card, dated 1907, was published by D. John, Stepney Street, Llanelli.

Class 3

A W. H. Smith card, postmarked 1915, of Felin-foel church and weir. *Class 3*

A Vaughan Evans card, *c.* 1905, portraying the family posed on the steps of Felin-foel House.

Class 6

The Quarry, Furnace.

A rare 1905 card of the stone quarry at Furnace, Llanelli. The steam crane, behind the buildings, and the barge in the foreground are clearly visible.

Class 2

50

Maes Canner Road, the bridge and church (far right) at Dafen, *c.* 1907.

A panoramic view of Dafen, postmarked 1912, published by Bryn Morgan.

Class 4

Victoria, a double Fairlie 0-6-6-0 loco, being worked on the Burry Port and Gwendraeth Railway, *c*. 1903. The loco is pulling coal waggons full of miners' families *en route* to Burry Port beach on a Bank Holiday outing. *Class 2*

The seaplane *Friendship* in Burry Port harbour, 18 June 1928. On board the plane, piloted by Wilma Stultz, was Amelia Earhart, the first woman to fly across the Atlantic.

Class 2

A Roman Catholic church service on the lawns of Pembrey House during Corpus Christi. The congregation includes soldiers and N.C.O.s (right). This rare 1917 card is by J. Harper.

Class 1

G.W.R. STATION
BURRY PORT.

Burry Port railway station, *c.* 1910. This W. H. Hoare card is possibly the work of Ernest T. Bush.

Class 2

Nine coal ships and a tug in Burry Port harbour, 1903. Note the wooden coal hoists in the background. *Class 4*

Station Road, Pembrey.

Station Hotel in Station Road, Burry Port, 1905, not Pembrey. The publisher got the location wrong!   *Class 4*

Upper Elkington Road, Burry Port, *c.* 1910. Many changes have taken place since this photograph was taken. *Class 4*

Behind the wall running alongside Church Road, Burry Port, stood an apple orchard and house, the property of a Mr. Chivers. The site is now known as Chivers Corner. St. Mary's Church is in the background.

Class 5

Station Road, Burry Port, *c.* 1926. The postcard was published by W. T. Perrott, owner of the shop on the right. The gable-end of Edmonds the ironmongers is clearly visible in the centre of the photograph. *Class 5*

A rare card by E. T. Bush of Tyle Teg, Burry Port, *c*. 1926. St. Mary's Church spire is visible in the distance. *Class 2*

A postman delivering mail in Ashburnham Road, Pembrey, 1927. Behind him is the ivy-covered Ashburnham Hotel. *Class 3*

Burry Port from the Pier.

A panoramic view of Burry Port, *c.* 1902 (from left to right): the Coffer Dam, Custom House, coal carrying sailing ships in the East Dock and a two-masted brigantine in the harbour.

Class 4

Burry Port, *c.* 1910. The small white building (right) is the Dockmaster's Office. The harbour light stands at the end of the Pier.

Class 4

Burry Port, *c.* 1913, busy with lots of pedestrians but cars are conspicuously absent. The bystanders outside London House (right) are determined to 'watch the birdie'!

Class 5

WITH GREETINGS FROM
PEMBREY CAMP S. WALES 1913.
PUBLISHED BY W. S. TUCKER. NO. 458

Troops camped at Pembrey in 1913 sent postcards, similar to this W. S. Tucker multiview card, back home.   *Class 4*

Towyn Farm, Pembrey, *c.* 1929. The farm stood on land which in 1937 became RAF Pembrey Fighter Command. *Class 1*

The old harbour Pembrey, built in 1819, as it was in 1916. The sandy area acted as a scouring basin used to flush silt from the harbour.   *Class 5*

A Francis Frith card, dated *c.* 1948, shows Edwards Terrace, Pembrey, and the humped-back road bridge over the Gwendraeth Railway.

Class 6

Y Graig, Burry Port, *c.* 1914. Alongside the unmetalled road can be glimpsed the old Farmers Arms. The card was published in Bath.

Class 2

Gwscwm Road, Burry Port, looking south-west, *c.* 1935. Many changes have taken place since this scene was recorded on camera.

Class 4

An unusual view of the old harbour Pembrey, *c.* 1904. How different Pembrey, not Burry Port as claimed by the publishers, looks today.

Class 2

Old thatched cottages in Pembrey village, *c*. 1910.

Class 3

The Square, Pembrey. 684.

A superb view of Randell Square and the Commercial Arms, Pembrey, in the days of horse-drawn traffic. The card is postmarked 1914.

Class 2

Edwardian passengers, including smartly dressed ladies, at Burry Port awaiting the arrival of the train to Carmarthen. The card was posted in November 1912.

Class 4

Gwendraeth Valley railway cards, such as this postcard dated *c.* 1920, are always in demand. The coaches (right) were old stock purchased from the Metropolitan Railway. In the background is the Neptune Hotel. *Class 3*

Servant girls posed outside Plas Newydd House, Burry Port, *c.* 1908.

Gwendraeth Valley rail staff posed in front of No. 12, 0-6-0 loco, built by Hudson-Clarke. This rare card by J. Harper of Burry Port is dated *c.* 1911.

Class 2

August Bank Holiday Monday, 1932. This camp, near Burry Port harbour, was established by local residents. The photograph was taken by Ernie Griffiths.

Class 1

80

The Docks, Burry Port.

Coal ships moored alongside wooden loading hoists in the East Dock, Burry Port, *c.* 1903. The card was published by the Excelsior Co., Carmarthen.

Class 3

Red Cross cup-winning team at Burry Port, 1942. Holding the cup is Mrs Megan Davies. Mrs. Muriel Snook, the captain, is seated on the right.

Class 1

These houses, built by Edward Goodwin, became part of Goodwin's Town, Burry Port. At the beginning of the century Pemberton Avenue's unique brick pavements led to open fields where today stands Glan-y-môr School. This rare card is dated *c.* 1906. *Class 1*

'The Lido', a romantic description of a crowded East Beach, Burry Port, *c*. 1934. Standing by the tent is Jack Mariti, a well-known local lifesaver.

Class 3

Harbour House, Burry Port.

Mr Arthur Morgan, General Manager of the Burry Port & Gwendraeth Valley Railway at Harbour House, Burry Port, in 1910.

Class 2

Burry Port Power Station in the process of being built in 1948. Locally it was known as the Carmarthen Bay Power Station.

Class 6

Bacus buses and taxis with their drivers posed alongside the vehicles outside the Gwendraeth Hotel (now the British Legion), Burry Port, *c*. 1936. The picture is by Ernie Griffiths.   *Class 3*

Stepney Road, Burry Port, *c.* 1912, complete with pram, lorry, motor bike, hand cart and fascinated onlookers. In the background is a stonecutter's yard.

Class 2

88

Copyright
Pby. 15
Pembrey School Camp (b).
Raphael Tuck & Sons Ltd
London.

School children enjoying a summer school-holiday camp at the Royal Ordnance complex, Pembrey, in 1935. *Class 4*

Llanelli GWR station in 1912. The first motor spare wheels were manufactured by Davies Bros. in the building to the right of the station.

Class 4

A Vaughan Evans card, postmarked 1904, of Lower Goring Road, Llanelli.

Class 2

Troops of the Sussex Regiment on stand-by duty during the 1911 rail riots in Llanelli. They were camped on the Railway Field, Burry Port.

Class 1

Pwll, Llanelly

The pool (*pwll*) and houses of Pwll village, near Llanelli. The card is postmarked 1906.

Class 4

Cilymaenllwyd house (later a hospital), Pwll, 1916. It was the home of the Rees family during the 1840s. *Class 5*

Hand-cranked Shell and BP petrol pumps at Gwalia Garage, Cross Hands, near Llanelli, in the 1920s. *Class 1*

The old Spudders Road bridge, near Trimsaran, is no longer in use but stands as a reminder of former coaching days. Since this photograph was taken in the 1930s there have been many changes. *Class 6*

The Square, Pontyberem.

Pontyberem Square, *c.* 1934. Alongside York House (left) stands an unusual white telephone kiosk. On the opposite side of the road is the impressive ironmongers shop of Harries & Walters.

Class 4

Two men pause to gaze at the photographer in Trimsaran's main street. The card is postmarked 1950. *Class 2*

A fine body of soccer players at Trimsaran, 1917. But where's the football?

Class 3

A multiview card of Pontyates, postmarked 1920.

Class 3

It appears that all the residents of Pontyberem had turned out to attend the local agricultural show in *c.* 1907.   *Class 3*

A wonderful view of Llannon recording for posterity some of the local children and other residents. *Class 2*